LESSONS LEARNED
FROM ATKA

Written by Lois Kral
Artwork by Melissa Fischer

Briley & Baxter Publications | Plymouth, Massachusetts

ISBN: 978-1-954819-42-9

Book Design: Stacy O'Halloran

DEDICATION TO ATKA

The wolf that would change the world and my life.

Atka arrived at the Wolf Conservation Center on May 24, 2002, at only one week of age. At a mere two pounds, he quickly won the hearts of the small team that would care for him for the next sixteen years.

Very early on, his curious and confident nature was very apparent. He would go on short, local excursions to the post office or around town and clearly embrace seeing new places and meeting new people. Very atypical behavior for a wolf! Little did we know that this would be the foundation for a 16 plus year career of fulfilling the role of the Wolf Conservation Center's top educator. Over the years, Atka visited schools, libraries, and nature centers including a few visits to the nation's Capitol, serving as a true ambassador to his wild kin and beyond. Throughout his life, whether at home or on the road, Atka changed minds and inspired everyone he met. I had the immense privilege of working for and with Atka for his entire life. He shaped me as a person and contributed to who I am today. Atka has left his everlasting mark on this world and our hearts.

Rebecca Bose
Curator, Wolf Conservation Center

Anyone who met Atka fell in love with him,
A majestic, bold white wolf from the North.
By being who he was, a wolf, wild and free,
He taught us so many things we can be.

His howl was strong, unique, his own.
It was his song, his tenor, his part.
When we listened to his voice, the sound of the wolf,
It sailed from the trees into our heart.

To accept who we are and not what others think,
To believe where we are, we belong.
It is our job to live, not by others to judge.
Atka taught us to "sing our own song."

As Atka grew up, his coat turned white.
His eyes became yellow and bold.
All you needed to do was look into his eyes.
You could see Mother Nature's inner soul.

As Atka grew, he travelled many places,
Some quite far to roam.
Like Washington D.C., Syracuse, and New York,
He was always very happy to come home.

He showed us how to appreciate everyone he met.
Up and down the stairs he would climb,
Never wishing, never wanting to be somewhere else,
Just enjoying his experience every time.

Atka found joy wherever he went.
His world was a wolf's treasure chest.
He loved to run and swim and play in the snow,
Always appreciating Mother Nature's best.
He was one who accepted life as it came,
Enjoying its many high and low tides,
Showing us that life is to always be enjoyed.
So, dive in and enjoy your journey's ride.

Atka didn't care if you were tall or thin
Or broad where you didn't wish to be.
If you had a kind heart, were gentle and sincere,
He knew you were someone he'd like to meet.

What Atka taught us goes beyond our words.
It's how we act towards each other, not what others say.
To be kind, respectful, and honest to all,
He and his pack taught us this every day.
Atka taught us to be gentle, to respect what nature gives,
To listen to each other's song.
If we could only follow the guidance he gave,
Truly, we could finally all get along.

Atka was a special wolf.
His mark was clear and true.
Protect wildlife and his fellow wolves,
His hope is that you will, too.

The Wolf Pack Credo is what he lived.
Every line is what he embraced.
May we all take heed and listen to his heart,
And may this world become a better place.

The Wolf Pack Credo

Respect the Elders,
Teach the young,
Cooperate with the pack,
Play when you can,
Hunt when you must,
Rest in between,
Share your affections,
Voice your feelings,
And above all,
Leave your mark in this world
To make it a better place.

ABOUT ATKA

Atka was an Arctic Gray wolf born on May 17, 2002 and died on September 22, 2018. He was the travelling ambassador wolf for the Wolf Conservation Center in South Salem, New York. During his lifetime of sixteen plus years, he travelled through many eastern states, visiting thousands of schools, libraries, and an insurmountable number of community events. This special wolf was known not only regionally, but also nationally and globally. Atka's positive message of creating a better place for all, including his fellow wildlife, will uniquely ring true in all our hearts.

Photo credit: Rebecca Bose, curator at the Wolf Conservation Center

ABOUT THE AUTHOR

Lois Kral has volunteered as an educator and animal care specialist at the Wolf Conservation Center (WCC) since 2006 where she has helped raise three of the ambassador wolves and assisted the curator in taking care of Atka. Lois travelled with Atka on his roadtrips through his teaching adventures, as well as his experiences with programs at the WCC. Watching him all those years has given her a perspective that is as unique as it is rare.

Lois is a retired public music educator of thirty-five years and lives with her cat, Macy Jane, and horse, Mexico.

ABOUT THE ARTIST

Melissa Fischer grew up in rural New York, spending much of her youth roaming a nearby wildlife sanctuary or playing with her dogs, cats, and other pets. Through these happy hours immersed in the world of nature and animals, Melissa developed a strong love for the natural world and its inhabitants. She has sketched and painted while traveling and hiking in various regions of the United States, especially in National Parks, and has been Artist-in-Residence at Acadia National Park. Melissa particularly enjoys sketching from life and has filled many pages with sketches of Atka and other wolves at the Wolf Conservation Center.

ABOUT THE WOLF CONSERVATION CENTER

The Wolf Conservation Center teaches people about wolves, their relationship to the environment and the human role in protecting their future.

Founded by Hélène Grimaud in 1999, the Wolf Conservation Center (WCC) is a 501(c)(3) not-for-profit environmental education organization working to protect and preserve wolves in North America through science-based education, advocacy, and participation in the federal recovery and release programs for two critically endangered wolf species - the Mexican gray wolf and red wolf. The WCC's three education wolves reside on exhibit where they help teach the public about wolves and their vital role in the environment. Through wolves, the WCC teaches the broader message of conservation, ecological balance, and personal responsibility for improved human stewardship of our World.

Wolf Conservation Center, PO Box 421, South Salem, NY 10590 / nywolf.org

20% of all sales of this book will be donated to the Wolf Conservation Center and its mission.